Speed Reading

How To Enhance Concentration And Improve Focus, Accelerate Reading Rate, Enhance Memory Retention, Expedite Learning, And Increase Productivity Within A Time-Efficient Framework

Anatoly Grishina

TABLE OF CONTENT

Enhancing Reading Speed: Unlocking The Secret 1

"The Persistent Practice Of Speed-Reading: Strategies For Consistency 15

Intuition 37

Eye Exercises To Improve Your Speed Reading Skills. 79

Reading: The Science Of It 85

Speed Reading Is Beneficial For Cognitive Development 132

Enhancing Reading Speed: Unlocking The Secret

As aforementioned, the development of proficient reading capabilities at accelerated rates heavily relies on the refinement of motor skills. This specific skill entails the utilization of hand-eye coordination to effectively comprehend text at accelerated rates, serving as the pivotal factor in achieving faster reading capabilities. It is an established reality that the majority of individuals do not engage in manual reading, consequently contributing to a range of difficulties they encounter, including fixation, sub-vocalization, and regression. Fixation entails pausing at unfamiliar words or phrases, sub-vocalization involves the movement of the lips or internalized voice while reading, and regression refers to the act of re-reading previously covered material due to perceived lack of comprehension.

This book predominantly relies on the act of quickly scanning a single page within a time frame of ten seconds or less, employing the use of one's hand as a guiding mechanism for visual movement. This approach is advocated for three primary justifications:

1) It develops visual acuity for identifying unfamiliar words on a consistent basis. This effectively deals with the matter of fixation. In the absence of employing our hand as a reference, our visual perception will consistently encounter interruptions whilst trying to comprehend unfamiliar phrases and words. Frequently, we possess comprehension of these phrases and words; however, our inclination towards comfort often prompts our brain to intermittently decelerate its

processing in order to ensure accurate understanding of the written content. Nevertheless, by utilizing your hand as a central point of focus, you will be compelled to maintain a continuous motion, thereby developing and conditioning the muscles of your eyes to adapt to swifter movements.

2) It facilitates accelerated visual processing, enabling rapid reading without the occurrence of sub-vocalization. There is no need for us to visually observe a cup of black coffee and verbally express our thoughts in order to comprehend. The matter at hand is that, due to our acquisition of reading skills, we have become exceedingly habituated to the practice of sub-vocalization, which has become deeply embedded in our psyche in a negative sense. The methods discussed in this book will promptly eradicate this issue, all the while allowing for a

comprehensive understanding of the material just read.

3) It facilitates the development of your visual acuity to smoothly trace words from left to right, ensuring that no words are inadvertently overlooked. This stands in stark contrast to certain reading techniques I had previously acquired, which proved ineffective as they failed to enable me to take in the complete breadth of a page, from one margin to the other. This was counterproductive. The techniques that prove to be highly efficacious facilitate the rapid scanning of an entire page within a time frame of ten seconds or less, eliminating the necessity for regression.

Comprehension Issues

I have placed significant emphasis on the attainment of speeds averaging around ten seconds per page, which may lead one to ponder, "How am I expected to comprehend the content when reading at such a rapid pace?" By what means is that feasible?

The construction of Rome did not occur within the span of a single day. When engaging in the utilization of the presented speed reading techniques, it is likely that you may experience a decrement in your comprehension ability. It is indeed a pivotal component in the acquisition of the skill of speed reading.

Speed Reading Techniques

The mastery of effective speed reading techniques is crucial in order to achieve the desired outcomes. Individuals can ascertain considerable advantages from the utilization of crucial speed reading techniques, thereby acquiring the keys to successful reading through diligent practice and implementation. The critical aspect is to comprehend the objective of each technique and subsequently endeavor to accomplish said objective. It is indisputable that individuals have the capacity to enhance their reading velocity and comprehension skills to reach a range of 700 to 900 words per minute. However, prior to considering such a compelling data point, it is important to bear in mind that achieving it necessitates the implementation of regular training and the utilization of empirically validated methodologies. If you are seeking clarification on this matter, it is important to understand that there is a wide array of techniques available to enhance one's speed reading abilities.

However, it is crucial to note that only the proven and reputable set of techniques will yield desired outcomes, and it is these techniques that will be expounded upon in the ensuing discussion.

Prior to delving into the techniques, it is imperative to create an optimal reading environment. Allow us to briefly examine these preliminary measures

● Establish the purpose of engaging with a specific written material. You should deliberate upon the REASON behind your perusal of this text. Possible alternative phrasing in a formal tone: "Potential forms of written media include newspapers, magazines, novels, poetry collections, and personal correspondence." Ensure that you have a clear understanding of the intended purpose for engaging with the particular written material. It holds significance as one's interest in reading it will only be piqued once the objective is understood.

• Eliminate any potential distractions prior to engaging in reading. Silence your phone. Concentrate on emptying your mind of any extraneous distractions. Please switch off the television and select a location where silence is so profound that one can hear a pin drop. You may also kindly request those in the vicinity to maintain a distance for a certain period of time.

• Assume a comfortable seated position and commence from the title page. It is imperative that one consistently remembers to peruse the text inscribed within the cover. It will provide a comprehensive understanding of the book's content.

Now is an opportune moment to discourse on the various speed reading techniques individually:

Use a Pointer

A pointer can take the form of either a writing instrument, such as a pencil, or the tip of one's finger. The purpose of the pointer is to direct the movement of the eye. The brain bears responsibility for instructing the eyes to track the motion of the object. When the cursor is displaced across the text, the cerebral cortex actively compels the visual organs to track this displacement.

Please be aware that it is not advisable to manipulate the pointer at a rapid pace initially. Tailor the motion in a practical manner to accommodate your present pace of reading. Gradually elevate the rate at which the pointer moves throughout various stages of the practice session.

In addition to directing the movement of the gaze, the pointer serves as a crucial mechanism for accomplishing another fundamental task. The task of maintaining one's gaze upon the page poses challenges for a majority of individuals. Even the most minute distractions divert one's attention from the text. The cursor maintains visual attention on the page and limits cognitive distractions.

Avoid Sub-Vocalization

We have previously addressed the concept of sub-vocalization as we elucidated the intricacies of the reading process. In brief, it entails the act of mentally perceiving the sound produced by a word when reading it. Researchers have unveiled that the act of sub-vocalization is a phenomenon stemming from an individual's inclination to audibly read during their early years, typically during their school-age period. The neural pathways in the brain become acclimated to the phonetic patterns of words, resulting in their continued activation even during silent reading.

Sub-Vocalization hinders speed reading. It is crucial to silence the mental noise during the process of reading. There exists a singular technique of utmost credibility in order to circumvent sub-vocalization. It is a straightforward yet efficient approach; merely adjust the velocity of the pointer's movement to slightly exceed the rate at which your mind verbalizes the word. This straightforward suggestion yields favorable results, although it requires a significant time investment to ensure its proper implementation. Do not be discouraged by immediate lack of success. Devotion and discipline will yield favorable outcomes.

Please take note: It is crucial to always acknowledge that the mind actively articulates the words you encounter as you read. Once you are aware of this, only then can you deactivate it by rapidly adjusting the pointer.

Do not attempt to exceed the speed limit.

It is important to bear in mind that speed reading does not solely entail reading rapidly. It is imperative to remain cognizant of one's limitations and strive for gradual improvement, instead of harboring unrealistic optimism.

Always remember the objective. However, it is important not to disregard the factor of velocity. The objective is to closely monitor the velocity, document it throughout the practice session, and make note of any advancements. Once again, the role of pointer speed becomes apparent. Scientists have disclosed that, with repeated training, the brain adapts to the velocity of the cursor. The crucial aspect lies in the management of the pointer velocity, refraining from attempting to exceed the velocity at which eye movements occur. The most effective means of determining your potential speed is by observing the rate at which you become fatigued. Once you begin to experience fatigue, promptly reduce the pace and deliberately decelerate by adjusting the speed of the indicator.

Please be aware that if a point is repeated, you have the option to accelerate the pace of the discussion in order to serve as a reminder for readers. In this particular circumstance, one can optimize efficiency by smoothly gliding the pointer across the lines.

Always prioritize retention without making any concessions

Retention pertains to the process of committing pertinent information within the text to memory. It is imperative to bear in mind these crucial facts, as failure to do so would render the objective of reading unattainable. On certain occasions, it becomes necessary for individuals to adopt a more deliberate pace in order to give due focus to critical declarations, conversations, and statistical information. It is recommended that the reader acquires the skill of regulating their reading speed. They must possess knowledge of strategic scanning techniques, areas to expedite their reading pace, and sections that warrant a deliberate slowdown for optimal comprehension and retention of significant details.

"The Persistent Practice Of Speed-Reading: Strategies For Consistency

Speed-reading can provide various benefits in a frontline context, be it within a professional setting during regular working hours or in an academic context for college students preparing for final examinations. If one cultivates the practice of speed-reading, it has the potential to greatly enhance one's professional and personal advancement. Through the act of reading, one can acquire a wealth of knowledge and maintain a consistently engaged mind, fostering personal growth and creating opportunities for enhanced achievements in life.

The additional knowledge acquired through enhancing your reading speed has the potential to elevate your performance in the workplace, positioning you as a stellar employee and paving the way for career advancements. With the new knowledge you have acquired, it is highly likely that you will be able to secure a substantial increase in your salary. Indeed, you can undertake a program of study to enhance your skills and simultaneously allocate sufficient time for other commitments. Indeed, speed-reading possesses the potential to confer upon you an advantageous invincibility in your pursuits.

Considering this perspective, it is likely that you will experience a heightened sense of motivation to engage in daily speed-reading practice.

Methods of Speed-Reading

Whether you are seeking to acquire knowledge from your philosophy textbook or simply perusing the morning newspaper, it is undeniable that reading can become monotonous at times. Consequently, it is advisable to acquire the skill of rapid reading in order to expedite your tasks. Increased speed when reading may lead to a reduction in comprehension; nevertheless, with dedicated practice, one can mitigate some of the negative impacts associated with this.

Learning to Speed Read

Cease engaging in self-conversation, specifically by refraining from subvocalization. One method of preventing this behavior is to engage in gum-chewing or lightly press a finger against your lips if you have a proclivity for engaging in lip movement. The act of engaging in subvocalization may assist in the retention of information; however, it is also a significant contributing factor to augmented time intervals.

Develop the ability to discern the appropriate objects of focus and minimize any sudden, unsteady motions. This can be achieved by utilizing index cards which are adorned with X markings.

Maintain a speed that exceeds the capacity of your cognition, all the while utilizing an instrument that can direct you along the written material.

Skimming Text

Although skimming may not be the optimal approach for comprehensive studying purposes, it can be an effective method for quickly perusing newspapers and similar texts. It imparts only a superficial comprehension of the material.

Commence by perusing the titles and subheadings of the periodical.

Please proceed by perusing the introductory and concluding sections of the text. Ensure that you are not proceeding at an excessive pace, thereby enabling a comprehensive understanding of the subject matter.

Circle the keywords. In order to enhance your comprehension, it would be beneficial to peruse the text once more, specifically noting recurring words, pronouns, and any unfamiliar vocabulary. You may emphasize their role in enhancing your comprehension of the subject matter.

Please observe the images and diagrams provided. In a matter of microseconds, they can convey far more information to you than written text.

In the event that you become disoriented, we recommend referring to the initial sentence of the paragraph as it will assist you in comprehending the main topic.

Use annotations. As you progress, please annotate the significant terms and ensure they are words that provide a comprehensive understanding of the entire context.

Time Yourself

One can enhance their speed-reading skills in a more refined and authentic manner by consistently tracking their progress during reading sessions and purposefully accelerating their reading pace. Determine your reading speed by conducting a self-assessment over a 10-minute period. Calculate the number of words you read by multiplying the number of pages by the average number of words on each page, and then divide the total by 10 to obtain your reading speed in words per minute. Gradually increase your reading speed while focusing on a specific goal.

3. Memory Retrieval

The challenges faced by numerous individuals in accessing information are primarily attributed to the adoption of an inadequate retrieval methodology. Recollections are retained in various regions of the cerebral cortex, and upon attempting to recollect information, these distinct cortical areas are stimulated. For instance, suppose you are attempting to recall the color of the cover of a captivating book that you have read. Initially, you will generate an internal visual representation of the book, thereby engaging your visual memory. Subsequently, you will recollect the action of leafing through the book's pages, thereby activating your auditory memory, while simultaneously encountering intriguing information or even visuals within its contents.

Additionally, you might recall the previous occasion when you physically grasped the book, engaging your kinesthetic sense, as well as the emotional response elicited by the information contained within it. Alternatively, you may recall the scent emitted by the book as well as the ambiance of the particular setting in which you were engrossed in the reading experience, known as the olfactory milieu. When information is stored in this manner, it may substantially facilitate the process of recollection, given the abundance of associations that can be formed between the book and various elements.

Individuals retain information pertaining to vocabulary and engage in cognitive processing to interpret the significance of said vocabulary through the neural activity in the brain's left visual cortex. This is the process by which written words are graphically depicted as various elements, and the information that is read is committed to memory and transformed into narratives, communications, thoughts, abstract notions, and visual representations. While immersing yourself in the act of reading, it is advisable to stimulate the neurons in your brain, allowing vivid imagery corresponding to the text to inundate your thoughts, while establishing meaningful connections between the words, sounds, colors, and emotions that are contextually relevant.

Several cognitive strategies that can enhance your ability to remember and understand the information you read comprise:

1. Multiple Reading Process/Repetition

This entails a repetitive procedure encompassing previewing, providing an overview, and actively engaging in reading the information you aim to retain in your long-term memory. The procedure necessitates a preliminary examination of the material prior to note-taking. After conducting a preliminary review and jotting down notes, it is advised to reexamine the material and take additional notes. The next step entails thoroughly perusing the information and, if desired, making annotations. It can be likened to reiterating the information six times without thoroughly perusing it beyond a single instance. It is nonetheless crucial to acknowledge that the process of repetition is not a significant time-consuming factor in your reading.

Presented below is an overview of the various reading procedures:

Preliminary examination: Familiarize yourself with the introductory details, peruse the opening sentences of each paragraph, and scrutinize the concluding remarks while making detailed annotations. The preview offers the reader a comprehensive perspective on the contents at hand. Upon gaining a comprehensive understanding of the content, you will subsequently be able to peruse it with greater efficiency.

Summary: Familiarize yourself with the introductory sentences in each paragraph, as well as the headings, subheadings, and any emphasized words, and proceed to make concise notes.

Peruse: Peruse the complete text and subsequently make concise notes.

In the majority of instances, individuals peruse the complete discourse or literature devoid of repetition, subsequently encountering difficulties in recollecting the content the following day. This arises primarily due to the fact that they were only exposed to the material on a singular occasion. Through active participation in various reading processes, one can enhance their ability to retain information by virtue of the considerable repetition involved. The practice of repetition is vital for solidifying information in long-term memory; to ensure retention, one must partake in a multitude of repeated exposures.

An alternate method to achieve repetition of the information you have read is through engaging in discussions with another individual regarding the content you have perused. When you put the information you have read in your own words, you tend to remember it for a longer period of time.

1. Visualization

Visualization can also serve as a mnemonic technique, as individuals tend to have greater ease in recalling information that they have mentally visualized. This is the rationale behind why a significant number of individuals have a propensity for recalling individuals' visages as opposed to their names. If one is capable of mentally picturing the information while reading, it can significantly enhance one's ability to recall the information at a later time. Make a conscious effort to engage in visualizing the information you are reading, and endeavor to do so after completing each section or paragraph.

2. Exaggeration

Additionally, this method encompasses the process of conceptualizing and retaining non-conventional stimuli as a means of encoding and recalling information. For instance, while mentally processing the information you are perusing, you have the option to amplify or diminish the data by magnifying or reducing its magnitude within the confines of your thoughts. Engaging in such practice will aid in the effortless retention of the information, even upon a subsequent occasion.

3. Association

Utilizing the principle of association serves as an alternative method for retaining and recalling information. By forming connections between the information you have read and existing knowledge, the process of recalling it in the future becomes significantly facilitated.

4. Chunking

An alternative method for improving memory retention of information involves employing the technique of chunking, particularly when faced with the task of comprehending extensive and intricate material. By dividing it into smaller components or segments, you will enhance your reading comprehension. For instance, when perusing a chapter comprising five pages, one can segment the information into more manageable sections in order to leverage additional memory techniques for effortless retention.

Managing Technical Terms

Typically, when engaging in reading, individuals are likely to encounter certain technical terms whose meanings may not be immediately apparent. Consequently, there exists the potential for individuals to be diverted and experience a reduction in reading speed due to the presence of such terms. Rather than interrupting your reading to lookup the definition of a word, it is recommended that you proceed with reading and perhaps you will discern the meaning within the text itself.

Essential Strategies for Achieving Speed Reading Proficiency

Irrespective of your existing reading pace, there exist several methodologies and approaches that can be employed to enhance your reading speed. However, it should be noted that possessing knowledge of these strategies alone might not suffice in yielding significant benefits, as neglecting key fundamental guidelines can hinder the effectiveness of your speed reading endeavors. Listed below are several strategies that can be employed to rectify inadequate reading habits and enable effective engagement in practices that foster success in speed reading.

Unwavering Commitment to Practice: The acquisition of speed reading skills necessitates dedicating sufficient time and effort to practicing. Engaging in regular practice not only activates the brain, but also facilitates its involvement in facilitating the entire process. Engaging in the skill of speed reading additionally facilitates an accelerated assimilation and recollection of the subject matter at hand. Thus, practicing speed reading not only leads to an elevation in reading speed through diligent efforts, but it also amplifies one's capacity for understanding and retaining information.

Begin with simple material: To ensure consistent practice when embarking on speed reading, it is recommended to commence with reading materials that bring you pleasure. For instance, if one possesses an affinity for literary narratives, they may commence their exploration with storybooks, novels, periodicals, or any other literature of personal intrigue. As you peruse intriguing content, not only will you engage in honing your speed reading skills, but you will also derive pleasure from the process, particularly advantageous for those who are new to this endeavor.

Commencing your speed reading practice with an uninspiring subject matter can prove to be rather overwhelming, particularly for someone who is new to this skill. In instances where the subject matter is intricate, individuals often experience a diminished motivation to persist in their practice, resulting in a potential inclination to abandon their efforts and hinder their progress in the domain of speed reading.

Employing a Pointer or a pacer: Employing this uncomplicated device during reading can prove beneficial in mitigating challenges related to speed reading. A pacer or a pointer refers to any object, such as a pen, one's finger, a chopstick, or any item that can be used to indicate or direct attention to specific words while reading. There is sufficient evidence to support that employing pointers, such as employing one's hand or a pen, during reading can significantly augment reading speed. The utilization of a pacer serves to eliminate disruptions while simultaneously involving an additional sensory perception in the act of reading.

The utilization of a pacer or pointer serves to imbue one's reading with a kinesthetic quality, thereby augmenting the capacity for memory retention and recall. The utilization of the hand or writing implement can assist in directing one's gaze along the text while reading, thereby mitigating the occurrence of the eyes darting back and forth, a phenomenon which can occur during the process of reading. Consequently, the pacer aids in directing one's gaze, ensuring the focused engagement with the material being read. The utilization of a pointer can also serve as a straightforward method to assist in the regulation of one's focus while reading.

If one is able to attain a higher level of concentration, this will consequently result in an enhancement of both reading speed and comprehension. One can position their fingertips beneath the text being perused while transitioning smoothly from the left side to the right side. As visual attention is captivated by movement, it shall obediently track the motion of your fingers or the implement you employ, allowing you to effortlessly navigate through the textual content. Although the initial stages of the process may induce discomfort, with persistence and practice, one's familiarity will grow, allowing for a seamless and effortless execution.

"An overview of the advantages associated with employing a pacer or pointer:

Facilitates seamless and effortless transition to different segments.

Facilitates and enhances concentration on the material being read.

Assists in inhibiting sub-vocalization as focus transitions to the hand with the activation of the sense of touch.

Facilitates the process of speed reading by enabling the reader to perceive multiple words simultaneously.

Intuition

I have previously alluded to the fact that intuition can serve as a valuable instrument when conducting rapid analysis of individuals in your vicinity. It is a tool that I frequently utilized in my personal practice of speed reading. In the following chapter, we shall delve into the essence of intuition, acquire precise techniques for applying it effectively in the practice of speed reading, and explore a personal anecdote that aptly demonstrates the formidable power of intuition.

Firstly, we shall delve into the true essence of intuition. Intuition can be described as an innate perception or insight that arises regarding a person or situation, even in the absence of substantial information. The emotional response that may arise evokes either a sense of peril or a sense of security. It is not inherently an acquired proficiency; rather, it is primarily an innate attribute.

As a result of this, intuition can prove to be a formidable asset when it comes to engaging in the practice of speed reading.

When applying intuition in the context of speed reading, it is employed in a similar manner to its application in any other context. Employing intuition while observing individuals in your vicinity bears a resemblance to the application of intuition in other facets of your existence. There may not be an inherent requirement for you to actively rely on your intuition. It is a phenomenon that occurs instinctively.

As a result, intuition cannot be relied upon as a dependable instrument. It does not qualify as an implement suitable for inclusion in your inventory of resources. Occasionally, it may occur to you whilst discerning an individual's character, while at other times, such an insight may elude you.

The paramount consideration when employing intuition during the process of observing individuals is to consistently bear in mind its application once it manifests. It can be regarded as a tool that is exceptionally cost-effective. It is an inherent process that occurs effortlessly, and you can harness it to your benefit.

There is a specific occurrence in which my intuition proved to be helpful, and maybe even prevented harm, that remains prominent in my memory. During my collegiate years, I dedicated my summers to employment as a cashier within a horticultural establishment located in a rural community. The duration of the days was extensive, while the clientele proved to be scant, necessitating my investment of numerous hours in tending to the plants and anticipating the arrival of customers at the checkout counter.

Due to the limited workload, I frequently resorted to engaging in rapid reading of the individuals who frequented the establishment. I would endeavor to ascertain whether they were fathers of young children or individuals engaged in demanding professional occupations. I would envision the kind of garden that aligns with their individual personality traits. This not only aided in occupying my time, but also enhanced my comprehension of my clientele. Consequently, this facilitated my ability to provide enhanced assistance to the customers.

On a particular occasion, though, I found myself not needing to employ my speed-reading techniques in the slightest. The entrance to the garden center was unlocked, and an auditory indication of approaching individuals was noted through the sound of footfalls. My instinctual response ensued prior to my gaze being directed toward the newly arrived patrons.

By some inexplicable means, my intuition detected malevolence emanating from these individuals. I successfully activated the button on my register, signaling security to promptly attend to me before any potential issue could manifest itself. The gentlemen advanced directly in my direction, and the feeling of malevolence intensified.

The presence of security personnel was already established within the premises prior to the men's approach towards the cashier counter. Upon sighting the officers, the individuals promptly reversed their direction and exited the establishment.

In the given circumstances, my intuition was an instinctive reaction. It was an instinctual response by my physical being to safeguard myself from a potentially grave circumstance. It was fast, and I was not in control of this instinct. I was unable to contemplate the idea of speed reading these individuals due to the rapid activation of my intuition. Nonetheless, my body instinctively processed the negativity they brought into the establishment, resembling a reflexive form of speed reading.

Presently, this intuition was fervent, and generally, one's encounter with such speed reading will not be as heightened. One might perceive indications that an individual may require assistance in funding their grocery purchases, exemplifying the situation at hand. One might experience a sense of deception in a conversation with someone, thus perceiving indications of dishonesty. In due course, it is plausible that you may eventually experience intuition with a similar degree of intensity as I did, particularly within a high-stakes scenario.

Regardless of how intuition presents itself, it is imperative that one pays heed to it. It is evident that this tool is one of the most formidable resources for speed-reading at your disposal. It facilitates effortless usage as there is no need to retain any information; one can seamlessly tap into their emotions as they arise. While the usability remains straightforward, its efficacy is undeniably profound. It constitutes both a sentiment and an accelerated reading instrument that one must never disregard.

Furthermore, apart from safeguarding oneself from potential perilous circumstances, as it did in my case, one's intuition could also facilitate the preservation of those whom one is perceiving. I too have encountered this situation, albeit in a more recent context during a session with a client. I had the opportunity to provide care to an individual who was a mentally challenged war veteran seeking treatment for post-traumatic stress disorder (PTSD). Notwithstanding his post-traumatic stress disorder, he exhibited a generally contented and affable demeanor. I consistently experienced a positive sense whenever encountering him, and occasionally, his ability to conceal his underlying trauma, coupled with his susceptibility to being triggered by even the most innocuous of stimuli, rendered it challenging to recognize his distress amidst the façade of pleasantness.

On a certain day, he attended his biweekly appointment and an instinctual sensation in my core indicated that something was amiss. He extended his customary greetings to me and displayed no discernible deviation from his usual demeanor. However, I had a strong sense that there was a substantial issue with him. The sensation of malevolence I experienced on that occasion when those individuals approached me at the garden center was distinctively dissimilar. On the contrary, it gave rise to a sense of apprehension and an eerie premonition of an impending misfortune befalling him, rather than myself.

As the session progressed, no atypical incidents transpired; however, I remained unable to dispel that sensation. Ultimately, I concluded our typical dialogue and transitioned to inquire, in a more serious manner, if my patient had ever harbored any contemplations of self-harm. As per usual, he denied my request, but I persisted. My intuition persistently urged me to address this matter, therefore I resolved to persistently inquire with him until I attained a satisfactory understanding of the truth. Finally, he conceded to me that he had intended to take his own life immediately upon returning to his residence following our meeting. Despite experiencing internal distress, I successfully calmed him down and persuaded him to accompany me to the medical facility, where he could be admitted for psychiatric evaluation. He successfully sought the assistance required to navigate this challenging phase in his life, while I once again gained insight into the criticality of relying on my intuition in accurately assessing individuals.

Although not entirely infallible—there have been instances where my intuition has proven erroneous—intuition possesses significant strength and utility. You will not consistently possess the privilege of harboring doubt towards your intuition, particularly when it endeavors to caution you in times of emergency. Hence, it is advisable to cultivate the habit of prioritizing the guidance of your intuition, subsequently validating its accuracy through subsequent verification. It has the potential to preserve an individual's life.

For the exercise presented in this chapter, kindly reflect upon an instance where you availed of your intuition in your personal life, and proceed to articulate your account within the designated area below. This will facilitate your ability to discern the sensation of intuition, thus enabling you to readily identify it when its utilization as an expedient tool for rapid reading presents itself in subsequent instances.

May I inquire as to the method by which you achieve that?

There exists a multitude of methods to compute your words-per-minute (WPM) measure. Nevertheless, we have included three speed reading tests in the appendix of this book, spanning approximately 700 words, intended for you to evaluate your existing reading pace. These tests will serve as a benchmark to measure the progress you make by employing the techniques outlined in this book. Additionally, there is a comprehension test provided for every 700-word reading segment, which is located within the appendix of this book following each reading segment.

To evaluate your reading speed, commence by initiating a stopwatch and timing the duration it takes you to read a segment of text consisting of 700 words. Whilst perusing it, maintain your customary speed. Do not attempt to expedite your reading or strive to outpace time. We are evaluating your current level of reading speed. Subsequently, refer to the Speed Reading Rate chart that has been furnished towards the conclusion of this chapter and is additionally accessible in the appendix, so as to ascertain the duration of time expended in reading the aforementioned segment. Next, direct your attention to the adjacent column where you will find the measurement of your reading speed in words per minute. After determining your initial reading rate in words per minute, proceed to undertake the Speed Reading Assessment Test pertaining to the reading segment recently completed. Please respond to the test questions and subsequently verify your responses by consulting the answers provided in the appendix section that follows the assessment tests. Once more, it is imperative that you maintain honesty in this matter - it is strictly prohibited to revisit the text in search of answers. Each test consists of ten questions, and therefore, each question holds a weight of 10% in the overall evaluation. Consequently, provided that you have responded accurately to 8 items, your score equates to 80%. Please refer to the Speed Reading Rate table, locate your words-per-minute (WPM) rate, and proceed to the left to locate the column corresponding to your score on the Speed Reading Assessment Test. In that column, you will find your Effective Words Per Minute (EWPM) reading rate.

    We recommend utilizing your EWPM as the initial value. Why? We kindly request that you employ the methods outlined in this book to enhance your reading speed while also deepening your understanding of the material. Having a quick reading speed but lacking comprehension renders one's efforts futile. Our objective is to enhance your reading proficiency by increasing your speed and efficiency.

The typical reading speed for an average individual is approximately 200 words per minute. Any speed that exceeds 300 words per minute (EWPM) is regarded as noteworthy, while a speed reading rate of 700 EWPM or higher is considered exceptional.

Where do you stand? Average, below average? Please be assured that it is of no concern if you are. Commend the fact that you are embarking on the journey of self-improvement and acquiring a new skill! In the event that your score does not reflect a significantly exceptional level, there is room for enhancement (and we will provide guidance on this matter in subsequent chapters of this book!).

Furthermore, there is no need for concern if your words per minute (WPM) or effective words per minute

(EWPM) fall within the average range, as this is entirely typical. Indeed, the majority of individuals possess a typical rate of reading and level of understanding, and this encompasses even the most intelligent individuals. The majority of physicians, attorneys, and engineers do not possess an exceptionally rapid reading rate. Consider the immense potential that could be unlocked if each individual possessed a significant increase in their EWPM capability. Envision the possibilities and opportunities that await those who attain a higher rate of EWPM in their reading.

While your aspirations may differ from his, adopting the practice of speed reading will propel you towards the realization of your goals, be it in your professional endeavors or in exploring the intricacies of our ever-evolving world.

Gaining a superficial understanding

The practice of skimming allows one to swiftly acquire sufficient information from the textual material being perused, facilitating the determination of its relevance and applicability. Additionally, it aids in the removal of extraneous content that bears minimal relevance to the specific information you are seeking. Subsequently, you may revisit the text and peruse the pertinent sections once more. As one acquires the skill of skimming a page, the tendency to engage in sub-vocalization diminishes, as the limited time available prevents the repetition of words within the mind. With this objective in mind, by removing extraneous content and superfluous elements, your overall reading speed will experience a substantial and noteworthy enhancement.

Key words

Each sentence is comprised of certain pivotal terms that make up the essence of the sentence. By discerning these crucial terms, one can more readily comprehend the principal purpose conveyed in the provided sentence. These pivotal expressions correspond to the action words and subject words utilized in the sentence. Consequently, within the given sentence "The Company announced a significant change in its production policy", the comprehensive significance can be derived from the terms "company," "change," "production," and "policy." Therefore, the significance of the sentence is conveyed solely through four words, in contrast to the ten words used in the initial sentence. Listed below are several illustrative instances:

The topic sentence

Similar to how a sentence comprises significant terms, paragraphs likewise encompass topic sentences. The paragraph comprises a select assortment of sentences that encapsulate the essence and core concepts. By recognizing and discerning these sentences, one can swiftly comprehend the subject matter of the passage. Typically, a single topic sentence can be found within a given paragraph. Once you have discerned the topic sentence, you may choose to bypass the remainder of the paragraph.

Take for example, the preceding passage that you have only recently perused. Please swiftly maneuver your hand, employing the conventional technique, traversing the lines and descending through the paragraph. Could you please discern the topic sentence? This ought to be the subsequent statement: 'These represent a finite number of sentences that encapsulate the bulk of the concepts and significance conveyed in the paragraph'. The example sentences presented below contain a topic sentence which is indicated by a series of underlined dots, whereas the keywords within these sentences are denoted by a continuous solid line.

Formatting of textual content

Typically, printers organize paragraphs in a manner where the most pertinent keywords are positioned within the central portions of the lines. Therefore, adopting the practice of thoroughly focusing on the central sections while rapidly scanning the rest of the page can prove to be highly effective. Once you have discerned the topic sentence, you may then make a determination as to whether you wish to proceed with the remaining portion of the paragraph. By adopting this approach, you can effectively reduce the time invested in reading while directing your focus solely on the pertinent components.

Zigzag hand movement

Alternatively, one can employ a serpentine motion in skimming, in contrast to the vertical motion from top to bottom. The objective of this initiative is to broaden your attention as you seek out the central idea and crucial terms. Please transition your hand from the upper left corner of the page and proceed in a fluid manner towards the right side of the third line. Now, proceed to shift your hand towards the left and downwards, precisely onto the sixth line, while maintaining this coordinated motion for the subsequent actions.

Exercise

Please proceed with the act of opening the book on which you are currently engaged in your practice. The objective is to briefly peruse four pages by employing your hand as the designated pointing instrument. Please ascertain the topic sentence in each separate paragraph. Employ the hand movement that is most comfortable for your own personal preference.

Using a ruler

Additionally, employing a ruler can serve as a useful tool to assist you in the process of skimming. Position it slightly beneath the initial line of the page, and swiftly scan the line for the pertinent terms. Now, proceed to adjust the position of the ruler to the next line, and carry out the identical action as before.

Exercise

Please commence the process of accessing the book on which you are currently engaged in practice. The objective at hand is to swiftly peruse the consecutive four pages of the literary work employing the ruler as a guiding instrument. Please determine the main concepts expressed in each paragraph by identifying the topic sentences. To date, there exist three distinct pointing techniques at your disposal for swiftly navigating through a page. It is recommended to engage in and become proficient with at least one of them.

Interactive Reading" or "Engaged Reading

This session aims to impart the principles of active or dynamic reading. The strategies presented will aid in enhancing your reading comprehension rate.

Who's a dynamic reader?

An engaged reader may be defined as an individual who engages with literary works, scholarly articles, or periodicals with the objective of deriving value or meaning from them. Frequently, when perusing a magazine, one is not actively seeking specific information.

Nevertheless, on different occasions, you might engage in reading with the intention of augmenting your understanding in the specific domain with which you are engaged. In this particular scenario, you engage in the process of discerning the information that you deem to be the most pertinent, subsequently discarding any material that is deemed extraneous. Fundamentally, being an active reader entails reflecting upon the underlying objective of engaging with the text and ultimately furnishing the corresponding response. There exist multiple rationales for engaging with the text: conducting a comprehensive article appraisal, seeking a comprehensive outlook, augmenting one's knowledge, or deriving pleasure, comparable to reading a novel or a book of jokes.

Before reading

Presented below are the pertinent inquiries that ought to be contemplated prior to proceeding:

What is the objective of your engagement with the content?

What is the reason behind your desire to peruse that particular journal article, magazine, or book? Is there any correlation between this and your professional responsibilities? Are you seeking to procure pertinent information pertaining to your professional obligations?

What knowledge have you acquired pertaining to the subject you are currently perusing?

When you respond to this question, it will facilitate the further expansion of your existing understanding in relation to that specific topic. You will extrapolate existing information and integrate it with the new data, thereby facilitating the consolidation of significantly more comprehensive details than would otherwise be feasible.

During the reading

As you commence the act of perusing, it is imperative to undertake a reassessment of the content that lies before you. Presented below are a series of inquiries for your consideration:

What is the present subject matter being deliberated upon?

Please ensure that you have comprehended the primary subject matter of the present paragraph, as well as its correlation to the preceding passage.

What is the arrangement or structure of the material?

Take note of the arrangement of the information. There exist multiple approaches for the presentation of information, including but not limited to: prioritizing least significant information prior, prioritizing most significant information prior, demonstrating cause and effect, drawing comparisons, arranging chronologically, and so forth.

*Which information is relevant?

Peruse the paragraph, seeking out the pivotal terms and identifying the topic sentence. Subsequently, ascertain its pertinence in relation to your objective. Should it not be the case, you may opt to omit the paragraph without incurring any substantial loss of information.

What is the subsequent subject matter?

Attempt to anticipate the forthcoming information being presented. The objective of this exercise is to establish more robust associations in your memory, both with the content you have read and the existing knowledge you possess, thereby facilitating the assimilation of a greater amount of new information.

After

Have you obtained the information you were seeking from your reading? Have you obtained the responses pertaining to the inquiries you had formulated preceding the comprehension exercise? If such is not the case, what circumstances led to the unfavorable outcome?

What actions can be taken to enhance one's ability to critically assess information and choose the most suitable option? Responding to this inquiry will assist you in selecting more refined literary content that will aptly address your queries during subsequent instances.

Exercise

Please refer to the techniques presented earlier to read two pages from your practice book. Now, it would be advisable to pause and contemplate the information that has been presented to you. Please revert to the initial phase of this particular procedure and endeavor to systematically address all the inquiries. Furthermore, proceed to peruse an additional four pages from your assigned practice book, critically assessing your understanding of the aforementioned inquiries. Furthermore, analyze the benefit derived from the preceding examination.

How to Create Effective Purpose

It is not arduous to delineate your purpose with precision. It centers on logical reasoning above all else. Nevertheless, there exist several valuable principles.

Your initial assignment involves introspection regarding the purpose behind your engagement with the given material. What is the rationale behind your decision to procure that book, report, or magazine? What are your expectations and intended outcomes in perusing the material?

Are you inquiring about the resolution to a particular inquiry or endeavoring to find a remedy for a specific challenge? Define it in detail.

Would you be interested in enhancing your proficiency in a specific domain? To what extent do you aspire to develop and refine those skills? If you desire to maximize their potential, will you be prepared to dedicate the required amount of time? Perhaps you can gain proficiency by acquiring fragments of knowledge and focusing on critical information? Furthermore, consider whether you are able to entrust assignments to individuals possessing the requisite expertise. In doing so, you would exempt yourself from the burden of acquiring said knowledge. Zero reading... hmm?

Are you interested in expanding your knowledge and expertise? It is conceivable that the act of memorization may not be imperative in any way. What if one were able to ascertain the whereabouts of essential information, take note of it, and subsequently retrieve it as necessary?

Will you be delivering a presentation or a formal address? What are the main aspects or topics you intend to address? What specific objectives or knowledge are you seeking to acquire from the material you are currently perusing? Please take the time to record this important information by writing it down and creating a detailed list.

May I inquire if you are in the process of composing a report, a term paper, or conceivably a manuscript? It is advisable to commence the process with a meticulous outline prior to engaging in the research phase. As your knowledge base expands, it is imperative to further elaborate and amend your outline.

Are you reclining in bed with a literary work, endeavoring to unwind and induce drowsiness? There is certainly no substitute for the pleasure derived from immersing oneself in a quality literary work. Commence reading without concern for productivity. Relax, embrace, and greet the initial fatigue.

Do you happen to be preparing for an examination? What content should be addressed? What holds the greatest significance - lectures, textbooks, or any other educational resources? What types of inquiries are encompassed within this examination? Such as multiple choice queries, problem-solving tasks, questions pertaining to specific details, vocabulary assessment, as well as conceptual inquiries?

It is advisable that, while engaging in the act of Previewing textbooks (the Preview will be elaborated on in a subsequent section of this lesson), one should exercise increased vigilance towards any inquiries one might come across within chapters or at the conclusion of chapters or the book. It is imperative to peruse these prior to ascertaining your objective. The author is imparting significant information to the reader.

As an additional remark, I would like to introduce to you the most efficient and expeditious approach to achieving optimal study outcomes in situations where time is limited. Esteemed students from renowned educational institutions frequently employ this method discreetly. (Please keep this information confidential, if you don't mind.)

Turn the page...

CAUTION: Exercise Vigilance – Rapid Learning and Remarkable Achievements May Provoke Suspicions of Academic Dishonesty!

One advisable approach is to make every effort to acquire previous exams that encompass the subject matter pertinent to the upcoming test. First and foremost, it is advised to inquire with your instructor regarding the content and structure of the test in order to gain a comprehensive understanding of the key components of your study materials that warrant emphasis. Subsequently, candidly inquire whether you could have access to previous examinations. Contrary to expectations, certain instructors affirmatively state so. If the response is negative, endeavor to contact an individual who has previously completed this course, and request to borrow their examination. Ensure that the class was conducted by the same instructor.

Your forthcoming clandestine course of action entails the utilization of academic records. Class notes should be regarded with utmost importance as educators often discuss topics they deem significant, which are likely to be assessed in examinations.

One approach is to acquire written records from an individual with exceptional note-taking abilities and unfailingly attend all lectures. Yes, buy them. Should you choose to do so, you need not personally attend the lectures and can thereby allocate your time more efficiently. I know, I know. Attending is usually mandatory. You simply need to employ innovative thinking in this situation.

Take into consideration that during lectures, the instructor presents their discourse at an approximate rate of 150 words per minute, which is considerably sluggish in terms of information transmission.

You have the capability to read at a significantly higher pace. Furthermore, should the instructor diverge from the core topic intermittently and conduct the lecture in a manner lacking organization - a behavior occasionally observed among certain professors - you are squandering a significant amount of precious time while seated in the lecture hall.

Acquiring pristine, transparent, high-quality notes and utilizing them for educational purposes is undeniably an intelligent approach when one's schedule is constrained.

The next step in establishing an efficient objective consists of determining the desired level of comprehension and retention to be obtained from the reading material. Please bear in mind that it is impossible to recall every detail, therefore it is crucial to provide specific information. Take time with this. It has the potential to significantly reduce the amount of time spent during the reading phase.

A. What level of understanding is necessary in this context? If we were to conceptualize comprehension as a spectrum ranging from one to ten, with one denoting a basic grasp of the material's subject matter, and ten indicating a comprehensive understanding of the majority of concepts and ideas, to what level would you prefer to establish the benchmark?

B. What quantity and type of recall is necessary? An indiscriminate retraction wherein one can expound upon the general subject matter in wide-ranging terms. Would you like a precise recollection of names, numbers, terms, and phrases? Having a precise understanding of your desired information or recollection will yield the most optimal and precise outcomes.

Presented herewith are several levels of recollection to stimulate cognitive processing:

LEVEL 4: A comprehensive overview of the central concepts presented in the book.

LEVEL 3: The underlying concepts presented in each chapter, or in specific individual chapters.

LEVEL 2: Elaboration on the content provided within each subcategory of a chapter.

FIRST LEVEL: Elaboration of key information from the majority of paragraphs within a given subsection.

In conclusion, I would like to emphasize that upon fulfilling one's purpose, irrespective of its simplicity or complexity, one would have essentially perused the pages of that book. Done. Finished. Mission accomplished.

Now, before delving into the primary objective of this lesson, which is to acquire strategic reading skills for time efficiency, it is essential to address a fundamental query:

What, Really, Is Reading?

In the book Speed Reading Secrets, we present a formal definition of reading as follows: (1) reading is the act of perusing printed material with the objective of enhancing speed, comprehension, and retention, and (2) reading is an active endeavor entailing the deliberate pursuit of particular information aligned with one's purpose.

There exist essentially three distinct methods of reading. The first is...

LINEAR READING

The lower range of linear reading typically falls between 100 and 400 words per minute (wpm), representing a range wherein a considerable number of readers find themselves confined. We extensively discussed this matter during the first session of our instructional course.

This spectrum is predominantly governed by the SEE-SAY-HEAR-THINK principle, wherein individuals visually perceive the written words, recite them internally, audibly perceive their inner voice reproducing the words, and subsequently contemplate their connotations.

Why these four steps?

Simple. Primarily, we have been habituated to strengthen the words presented to us on the written page through our internal vocalization.

Additionally, our speaking capacity ranges between 100 and 400 words per minute. Inhabitants of rural Tennessee often engage in rapid verbal communication, attaining speeds of approximately 100 words per minute, while engaging in conversations with their fellow truck drivers at the nearby fueling facility. A broker present on the trading floor of the New York Stock Exchange, approximately 400 in number. John F. Kennedy unequivocally established a new record during the 1960s by delivering a speech featuring gusts surpassing a threshold of 500. However, John F. Kennedy was far from being an ordinary individual.

Furthermore, our auditory capacity also serves as a constraint when applying the see-say-hear-think principle. The auditory discernment rate represents the upper limit of our cognitive ability to comprehend information through auditory perception, specifically pertaining to the voice within our mind. Range: 475-500 wpm.

The intermediate range of linear reading falls between 500 and 800 words per minute. A majority of the reading performed by the speed reader occurs within this range. The quicker your pace, the more you compromise your vocal presence, leading to a shift towards a more visual and analytical approach in your reading. One observes the written text on the document, yet one omits the process of sound amplification, allowing the words to be directly absorbed by the mind where they are contemplated for their significance and grasped.

The underlying concept is that when one exceeds a reading rate of 500 words per minute, the inner vocalization mechanism experiences difficulty in matching the accelerated pace. It assumes the form of an incessantly whirling tape, wherein an increasing number of words surreptitiously evade scrutiny and are comprehended silently.

The upper limit for proficient linear reading falls within the range of 900 to 1,200 words per minute. This requires a significant level of self-assurance, as you have minimal awareness of any discernible "voice." Upon arrival, you have entered the realm of VISUAL LITERACY. An unfamiliar sensation upon initial encounter. Similar to engaging in comprehending the written material while practicing the act of reading.

On occasion, when I engage in the act of rapid reading of fictional works, the experience becomes analogous to that of observing a cinematic narrative. The narrative swiftly unfolds, projecting vivid visuals onto the canvas of my imagination, thereby imparting an astonishing level of realism. It is noteworthy that the level of comprehension is significantly elevated in this context.

Once the reading speed surpasses 1,200 words per minute, the reader begins to simultaneously process multiple lines of text, leading to a heightened comprehension of ideas and concepts rather than sequential language. Individuals with a natural proficiency for rapid reading, ranging from 1,500 to 6,000 words per minute, engage in this practice. Typically, they exhibit a predominantly inferior gaze as opposed to a lateral one.

Exceeding a reading speed of 1,200 words per minute is not an instructional focus within the curriculum of Speed Reading Secrets. The explanation is straightforward: Achieving stable outcomes is a challenging endeavor that demands significant exertion to approach a satisfactory level.

Nevertheless, it is not imperative that we confine ourselves to a reading speed of less than 1,200 words per minute when perusing written material. We have two additional methods of reading, the initial of which is referred to as…

Eye Exercises To Improve Your Speed Reading Skills.

Insufficient ocular strength can significantly hinder one's ability to achieve desired reading speed, despite diligent efforts. Fortunately, you have the capability to engage in certain exercises that will facilitate an expedited comprehension of the textual material, while also yielding a fortification of the ocular musculature. Some areas for improvement that can be focused on are as follows:

Exchanging fleeting glances or fleeting eye contact.

Our initial objective entails focusing on the thumb to thumb glancing technique, as it effectively targets the intrinsic muscles of the eye sockets that play a crucial role in peripheral vision. In this particular instance, the initial posture can be either standing or sitting, followed by directing your gaze directly ahead. Extend the arms laterally and subsequently elevate the thumbs in an upward direction. Now, you shall proceed with the subsequent step without rotating your head, merely shifting your gaze alternately between the two thumbs, completing this action approximately 10 times for each thumb. Please lower your arms to rest momentarily, and proceed to repeat these steps several times until completion.

Eye writing

For the purposes of this exercise, our objective is to enhance the mobility of our visual focus. It is important to note that in the practice of speed reading, it is not imperative to consistently read from left to right. Certain individuals achieve success by effectively mastering the technique of chunking to such an extent that they are able to simply progress downwards on the page. Consequently, the utilization of eye writing can aid in navigating diverse pathways. In order to achieve the desired outcome, it is necessary to direct our attention towards a distant wall, either situated at a substantial distance or positioned opposite to our current location within the room. Now, one can envision oneself inscribing their name or other textual content on the wall solely through ocular movements. You would assume the role of utilizing them as the instrument for your artistic expression and proclaim your desire to inscribe the name. One may also attempt to transcribe the text using either block lettering or cursive writing as a means to ensure the genuine effort made towards mastering the vocabulary.

Hooded eyes

This strategy is recommended for individuals seeking to ensure that their eyes appear calm and at ease. It is advisable to employ this technique whenever your eyes are in need of some respite. Regarding this matter, it is advisable to partially close the eyelids and concentrate on maintaining their stability by preventing any involuntary trembling. While directing your focus towards the eyelids, you will discover that a sensation of deep relaxation engulfs your eyes. While maintaining closed eyelids, it is crucial to direct one's gaze towards a distant object. This will assist in maintaining visual strength during periods of reading fatigue and contribute to their overall ocular fortitude.

Eye squeezes

This particular option should be considered if you are seeking a means by which to alleviate strain and tension in your eyes. Furthermore, incorporating added flexibility into the ocular muscles can effectively enhance the circulation of oxygen and blood to both the facial and ocular regions. This is an activity that will require approximately three minutes to complete, therefore please prepare accordingly. Once you feel prepared, take a deep breath and gradually allow your eyes and mouth to widen to their maximum extent. This will facilitate the elongation of all facial muscles. When expelling breath, it is necessary to tightly shut and compress the eyelids, simultaneously contracting the muscles situated in the neck, face, and similar areas. Take a moment to retain your breath while continuously exerting pressure for approximately 30 seconds, in order to fully elongate the target area. Perform this action multiple times and subsequently pause briefly before proceeding to repeat it once more.

Maintaining optimal visual acuity is one of the most effective measures to guarantee desired outcomes in the practice of speed reading. These suggestions aim to enhance the strength and agility of the ocular muscles, enabling a more expedient and robust reading experience. Additionally, they promote strategic intervals for rest, allowing the eyes to sustain their productivity and contribute to improved reading speed.

Reading: The Science Of It

Enthusiasts of literature globally can celebrate upon discovering a highly efficient method to accelerate the pace of reading. The identical sentiment may be experienced by individuals who experience discomfort whenever they are tasked with an activity that necessitates reading. The average person typically has the ability to read approximately 200 - 400 words per minute, starting from the moment they begin reading the words, mentally processing the phonetics, and visualizing the unfolding plot (in the context of reading a novel).

However, with persistent practice and adherence to effective speed-reading techniques, individuals can acquire the ability to read books and various materials at two, three, or even five times the average rate. It is worthwhile to consider the substantial impact that a mere doubling of one's reading speed can have on the efficiency of information consumption. The conventional approach to reading requires the individual to physically shift their gaze across a text, moving from left to right, in order to sequentially read the words. During this process, it is common for one's gaze to instinctively focus on a specific point within each word, which may serve as the pivotal element in enhancing one's ability in speed-reading.

The optimal recognition point, commonly referred to as ORP, denotes the specific focal point our visual perception seeks within each individual written word. Once your gaze identifies the ORP, your cognitive faculties promptly commence the rapid cognition and interpretation of the word and its semantic significance in a mere fraction of a second. Subsequently, as your gaze continues to track every word within the sentences, you begin to derive meaning from them. Subsequently, upon perceiving a punctuation mark with your eyes, your mind will instinctively generate a logical train of thought. Subsequently, your gaze seamlessly transitions to the subsequent words and sentences, culminating in the complete comprehension of the entire composition. This suggests that approximately 80% of the brain's activity is dedicated to seeking the Optimal Recognition Point (ORP), while the remaining 20% is allocated to the process of understanding the words. However, during the act of speed reading, one does not adhere to this identical procedure.

The Comprehensive Explanation of the Reading Process

In order to grasp the methods by which one can significantly enhance their reading pace while ensuring comprehension, it is imperative to gain an understanding of the underlying mechanisms of the reading process. Essentially, reading entails the mastery of language as its foundation, and it surpasses mere visual perception. Reading abilities typically begin to develop around the age of six in the majority of nations and social contexts. Subsequent to that juncture, a considerable span of time would transpire for a child to be regarded as an accomplished reader. In the initial stages of acquiring literacy, it is common for children to exhibit the inclination to vocalize their reading. They engage in this practice to transform the textual content into an oral manifestation that is imbued with greater familiarity to their auditory senses. Over the course of time, they gradually acquire the ability to engage in silent reading.

Printed or written text is comprised of graphical notations and delicate strokes. Hence, the perceived constraints associated with your sight pose a notable impediment to your reading process. One of the most prevalent techniques used in speed reading consists of utilizing your peripheral vision (which will be elaborated upon subsequently) to process larger segments of the page, and occasionally, the entirety of the page, as opposed to reading words individually.

For individuals who possess an ordinary level of reading ability and have yet to acquire the skill of effectively utilizing their peripheral vision to enhance reading speed, they rely on eye movements during the reading process. The acuity of vision is more pronounced in the fovea, the central region of one's field of view, compared to the parafovea or periphery situated approximately 1°–5° away from the central focus of vision.

The rapid and precise eye movements, referred to as "saccades," enable the swift redirection of your fovea to the words your brain intends to process with exceptional efficiency. Hence, it follows that the Oculomotor system, responsible for regulating eye movements, plays a critical role in governing the temporal aspects and order of engagement between the visual system and textual information. Your cognitive processes have a significant influence over the duration of fixation on each word and the timing of your eye movements to subsequent words. This control mechanism guarantees that every word enters your foveal vision at the optimal moment. This is the typical modus operandi of the reading process for the vast majority of proficient readers. In order to enhance your speed reading skills, it is essential to modify this procedure as well.

Chapter 7 – Enhancing Reading Speed and Efficiency

Why?
Think about it. Consider the extent of your daily reading endeavors. One's initial morning task might involve perusing the newspaper to stay informed about current global affairs. Subsequently, you delve into correspondences encompassing work assignments and associates. Subsequently, you discover yourself delving into various literary pieces, such as books, reports, letters, and proposals, which constitute your ordinary routine.

Upon examination, it becomes clear that reading is potentially the most frequently utilized skill in our professional endeavors. It's that important. We often fail to acknowledge its significance.

That is not to be expected. Considering the profound influence that reading exerts on our everyday existence and professional trajectories, it is imperative that we persistently strive to enhance this skill.

What is the significance of developing improved reading skills? It entails the act of increasing reading efficiency by simultaneously quickening reading pace while maintaining comprehension levels. Furthermore, it necessitates the abandonment of subpar reading habits, allowing you to effectively harness your speed-reading capabilities in order to enhance your overall productivity.

How We Read

What is your method for interpreting the word 'indeed'? How do you decipher the individual characters within words, consider their specific forms, and adeptly combine them to form a coherent sentence that is intelligible to you?

To put it frankly, reading is a sophisticated ability. According to experts, it is believed that each of our eyes possesses the ability to simultaneously focus on separate letters and symbols, with an interval of two characters. The human mind has the innate ability to combine and integrate these images into a cohesive representation of the reality being perceived through the act of reading. Such activity happens instantaneously as we go about zipping through the pages.

Inefficient Eye Motions

In the instance of individuals with slower reading abilities, they have a tendency to inadvertently concentrate on each word as it transpires, gradually progressing through every line. The average human eye possesses the inherent capacity to encompass a range of approximately 1.5 inches, presenting the capacity to apprehend approximately 4 to 5 words within that expanse.

Furthermore, it is evident that readers typically do not depend on their peripheral vision to perceive the text located on the outer edges of a line.

Overcoming this is simple. Moderate the intensity of your gaze while you read. One can achieve this by maintaining a calm facial expression while gradually widening their field of vision. The outcome will manifest as your enhanced capacity to perceive clusters of words. The era in which individual words are observed distinctly has now elapsed. Upon attaining a level of proficiency in this exercise, your eyes will naturally traverse the page at a considerably accelerated pace compared to the conventional norm. As you approach the conclusion of each line, your peripheral vision will seamlessly continue by effortlessly scanning the final groupings of words.

The principle of Meta Guiding

This methodology hinges upon the notion of visually directing the human gaze by means of indicators (such as a pen or one's finger), thereby accelerating the reading process across extensive texts. For the purpose of participating in speed-reading, it is imperative that your eyes possess the capability to meet the requirements of this skill. Meta guiding entails the depiction of imperceptible forms within a written composition, with the objective of expanding the perceptual scope. This resource is designed to assist you in developing your skills for speed-reading.

    One possible alternative way to express the same idea in a formal tone could be: "An illustrative illustration can be found in the act of employing one's finger or writing instrument to trace patterns on a designated page, with the intent of engaging the visual cortex and thereby enhancing one's visual breadth to encompass the entirety of a line. Furthermore, this process may extend to the level of imprinting the information into the recesses of the subconscious mind, enabling subsequent retrieval at a later point in time." Furthermore, meta guiding is purported to have the effect of diminishing sub vocalization, thus enhancing the pace of your reading. It promotes active engagement of your gaze, discouraging the tendency to superficially scan through the material, thereby diminishing comprehension and impeding effective utilization of memory.

Your Speed-reading Success

Acquiring the skill of speed-reading is merely the initial stage. You will need to conscientiously develop both your physical and mental abilities in order to excel. The key component in this situation is diligent practice, which cannot be overstated. Use this skill regularly. It required several years for you to acquire the skill of reading. Furthermore, it will require a considerable number of additional years for you to enhance your reading ability.

When commencing acceleration, it is crucial to bear in mind the teachings and recommendations previously delineated, and implement them accordingly. Additionally, it would be beneficial to document the advancement of your present reading pace in order to assess the outcomes and consequences of your study routines and exercises. You have the option to utilize a variety of online platforms that provide assessments for speed-reading skills.

WHY WE NEED LEADERS

In our present world, a scarcity of truly exceptional leaders persists despite our vast human population. Our current state is lacking the fundamental components that instigate individuals to envision and pioneer, with the aim of sustaining serenity and amicability, while fostering the development and broadening of entrepreneurial enterprises. This entire process begins with leaders, as they play a crucial role in shaping the desired atmosphere within both work settings and households. We must elevate leaders as they serve as the fundamental support not only for organizations, but also for families and communities. Numerous workplaces foster environments that elicit disinterest among employees. They come to work. They fulfill their obligations. Then they go home. Subsequently, upon arriving home to their familial unit, individuals experience a significant depletion of energy and a heightened sense of irritation. Presently, the spouse becomes disheartened and retires to bed in a state of discontentment. The sunrise prompts them to repeat the process once more. This might appear as an exaggeration, however, it is genuinely not. If this does not align with your sentiments, then you are among the minority in an environment characterized by favorable conditions, for which you should consider yourself exceptionally fortunate. However, one can observe the cascading repercussions that arise within our environment when we are deprived of exceptional leadership. I have no desire for my employees to perish while attempting to conclude their duties. I am inclined to prevent them from experiencing stress and consequent decline in their health. I desire for their happiness and prosperity. Employees who belong to this particular category not only enhance the overall image of the organization, but also elevate your standing as a leader. When employees experience a sense of contentment, security, inclusivity, and are able to freely express their viewpoints. This marks the point at which companies commence innovation once more, manifesting significantly amplified levels of production. It is time to bring about a revolution that will transform the world. Individual individuals will be assisted sequentially. It is imperative for you to internalize the notion that you have the potential to excel as a leader, both in your professional and personal life. By doing so, you will gain a fresh perspective on the world around you. You shall have the capacity to become the catalyst for the desired transformation, but the journey commences with your self.

WHAT WE\\\'LL COVER

Throughout the duration of our time together, I intend to provide you with guidance on cultivating a prosperous mindset. In order to achieve success, one must harbor a genuine desire for it. Cease postponing difficult tasks. Initiate regular patterns and practices yearn for acquisition of knowledge. Establish objectives and strive to achieve them, placing particular emphasis on the diligent pursuit of triumph through education. Whether it is related to finances, athletics, or one's occupation... The most effective approach to acquiring desired objectives is to study the strategies employed by successful individuals, once you have cultivated a mindset centered on achievement. We will elucidate the fundamental aspects of leadership, encompassing their distinctive traits and principles. Subsequently, we shall delve into an exploration of distinct personality profiles to foster comprehension of individuals in your surroundings. Moving forward, I am particularly enthusiastic about the subsequent segment, which I deem crucial for your understanding. I will demonstrate the process of integrating all the knowledge you have acquired thus far, as well as the methods of practical application. You will acquire the skill to discern various characteristics and effectively engage in communication with individuals possessing these traits. It is unexpected to discover that these are the foremost pieces of information that a majority of individuals are unaware of. Furthermore, this will assist in evaluating the individuals within your team and adapting your leadership approach accordingly to suit the given situation. The traditional methodology of a universal solution no longer holds validity. Contemporary leaders are required to demonstrate adaptability and flexibility. In my observation, a prominent hindrance to effective leadership resides in individuals possessing a self-centered mindset, which ultimately impedes their capacity to lead efficiently. As a leader, it is essential to recognize that it is not within your realm of influence to compel individuals to conform to your expectations. It\\\'s about them. You must feel at ease with adhering to their expectations. Subsequently, we will delve into the impact of leadership on companies and businesses. We will discuss the evaluation of individuals, including those who are not directly subordinate to you. We intend to thoroughly explore the significance of maintaining an open mindset and encouraging them to evaluate your capabilities. I am not referring to the scenario in which someone in a higher position assesses your performance. I am referring to the acquisition of genuinely candid feedback from the subordinates within your team. In the following segment, we shall delve into the aspects of establishing rapport, fostering motivation, and deploying persuasion amidst the prevailing levels of stress within the workforce. I aim to conclude the class by addressing stress management. Certain individuals may wish to dismiss this matter; however, it must be acknowledged that stress possesses the ability to spread from person to person. If you display indications of irritability and discontent, you will observe its corresponding impact on your employees. As a leader, you establish the atmosphere, and it is crucial for that atmosphere to remain positive in order to effectively retain the information. There shall be various tasks and engaging simulations throughout the course. This does not serve as a testing environment; however, it serves as an effective means to offer you valuable feedback. If you have successfully accomplished everything, then allow me to extend my congratulations. You possess an innate understanding of the qualities and attributes necessary for exemplary leadership. I possess the knowledge and expertise to instruct you on a comprehensive range of subjects. Nevertheless, ultimately, the possession of determination and motivation becomes imperative in order to put the acquired knowledge into practice. It is crucial to bear in mind the age-old adage that knowledge devoid of action equates to ignorance.

Theoretical Part

Bad Reading Habits

Were you aware that the reading speed of an average adult does not surpass that of a seventh-grader? The reading proficiency reaches its full development at that point and subsequently ceases to progress further as one advances in age. It is a prevailing circumstance that individuals, including those with tertiary education, may often not experience an enhancement in their reading speed throughout the course of their academic pursuits. The majority of individuals are unfamiliar with the term "speed reading" and have never encountered this particular topic. You will swiftly discern the benefits you have derived from perusing this book in your day-to-day existence.

There are several fundamental aspects of reading that are improperly executed. Please observe the following examples and endeavor to commit them to memory.

Bad habit no. One - analyzing each word individually.

The visual representation depicted below illustrates the typical manner in which an individual of average reading abilities comprehends written content.

One would observe the manner in which his gaze transitions swiftly between different words.

This particular reading methodology is characterized by its slow pace, owing to self-evident factors. In this given demonstration, our focus is directed towards each individual word, followed by a momentary pause before proceeding to the subsequent word. In practical application, this approach consumes a considerable amount of time and proves superfluous.

The human visual sense has the ability to perceive multiple words simultaneously. Experienced readers frequently process four or more lines simultaneously, thereby avoiding time wasted on individual word recognition. By employing the skill of reading with peripheral vision, individuals can attain accelerated reading speeds, a capability that is accessible to all.

Here's a quick math. Let us assume, as an illustration, that a solitary line of text consists of 15 words. In practical terms, employing this approach would entail focusing on each of these 15 words separately, resulting in 15 fixations within a single line. However, an adept reader has the ability to comprehend this line with a mere three to four fixations.

As time progresses, one's cognitive faculties and visual acuity become accustomed to the process of perceiving and comprehending individual words. The objective of this book is to recalibrate your perception of the text and enhance your receptiveness to information. There may be a probability of encountering difficulties in comprehension when you commence your practice, but there is no need to be excessively concerned about it. Over time, with persistent practice, your level of comprehension will enhance.

Now, let us observe how a skilled reader goes through this text.

It is evident that there is a reduction in fixations by a factor of up to three. This serves as an exemplification of accurate reading, wherein a reader engages in the practice of perusing multiple words within each given instance. Initially, this may consist of a mere two to three words, however, over time, with diligent practice, this quantity will expand. A subset of highly skilled readers possesses such refined visual acuity that they can decipher an entire line of text with a single glance. To commence, it would be advantageous for you to cultivate the practice of reading multiple words simultaneously, thereby fostering contentment.

Henceforth, endeavor to approach the material with a broader perspective, directing your attention to multiple words simultaneously. With regards to understanding, it is deemed satisfactory to maintain a comprehension level of

50% while engaging in practice. This percentage will likely increase as you continue to diligently practice.

Bad habit no. 2 – engaging in internalized word repetition while reading

The act of subvocalization or internally repeating words while reading is a widely prevalent phenomenon. This widely prevalent habit has its roots in early childhood, during the period when individuals acquire the skill of reading. At that particular juncture, it was imperative to engage in the deliberate utilization of internal word repetition for the purpose of comprehending the textual material. The issue arises when adult individuals persist in engaging in this behavior. What is the underlying reason for this detrimental behavior? This habit is unfavorable due to the discrepancy between the pace at which we mentally vocalize words and our ability to visually perceive and comprehend the written content. Consequently, this practice detrimentally impacts our rate of reading. Certain proponents of speed reading assert the necessity of completely eradicating subvocalization; nevertheless, I maintain that it should be minimized to its utmost extent. Henceforth, endeavor to engage in reading without allowing the words to resound within your mind. Attempt to visually apprehend the concepts and cogitations conveyed by the author.

Speed reading techniques are derived from the reading methodology known as Brain Reading. The human brain possesses an extraordinary capacity for comprehending and analyzing a tremendous volume of written material, surpassing our ability to articulate it audibly.

Allow me to provide an illustrative instance that demonstrates the superfluous nature of subvocalization. Examine the traffic signage, for instance. Upon observing them, it is not requisite for you to mentally iterate the significance of every signal so as to comprehend it. Upon encountering a sign indicating a pedestrian crossing, one can effortlessly comprehend its intended significance. It is unnecessary for you to engage in internal repetition of the phrase "pedestrian crossing" in order to comprehend its meaning.

Techniques for Enhancing Reading Speed: Tips and Strategies for Speed Reading

In the following section, you will be instructed on various approaches to enhance your reading speed.

Eliminate Reading Myths

There are individuals who consistently proffer excuses to abstain from reading on account of certain "data" they have encountered. In reality, certain statements included in the aforementioned information are inaccurate. If one's mind possesses such ideologies, their concentration while reading is likely to diminish, consequently impairing their ability to fully comprehend the text. This has a significant impact on your reading velocity. Let us now examine several prevalent misconceptions surrounding the act of reading:

Reading is linear

Prior to acquiring the skill of speed-reading, a majority of individuals perceive the act of reading as a sequential and sequential process. Consequently, one must commence reading from the beginning, progressing methodically through each word, sentence, and sequentially following the textual arrangement until arriving at the concluding word contained within the book. This is unacceptable and should be rectified.

In the process of book authorship, certain writers opt to postpone the composition of the initial segment until the latter stages of their writing, as opposed to proceeding in a linear fashion, constructing their book sentence by sentence and word by word. Reading is not linear. Abandon the notion that you are obligated to consistently read in a sequential manner.

Reading involves examining each word in a meticulous manner.

A significant number of individuals hold the perspective that this statement is unfounded. This is a skill that is imparted during early childhood education, where instructors educate children to recognize individual letters within a word, enunciate the syllables, and ultimately comprehend the entire word. There are alternative interpretations available. Speed-readers have the ability to comprehend or assimilate information in a rapid manner by processing phrases, sentences, or even entire paragraphs simultaneously.

Reading is a time-consuming and arduous endeavor.

This is very false. Reading can provide both pleasure and expedience. Speed-reading can be likened to participating in a car race, an activity characterized by heightened thrill and excitement, as opposed to simply engaging in a slow and leisurely drive.

Each component of a book holds equal significance.

This is an erroneous belief that a significant majority of individuals unquestioningly embrace. Certain books frequently contain an abundance of extraneous content, resulting in the dispersion of valuable material throughout the book or its final sections.

In the practice of speed-reading, individuals possess the liberty to bypass impractical content and promptly access the pivotal information. This can be likened to expeditiously advancing to the pertinent information.

Enhancing reading speed will result in diminished information retention.

Certain individuals hold the viewpoint that engaging in accelerated reading practices is accompanied by a trade-off in terms of both retaining information and comprehending the material. The utilization of reading strategies employed in speed-reading has the potential to enhance both your ability to retain information and your level of comprehension.

Determine Your Present Reading Rate

In order to record any enhancements in your reading speed, it is essential to evaluate your initial speed prior to implementing any speed-reading methods. Please find outlined below the procedures to assess your present reading velocity:

1. Select a book according to your preference and designate a point at which to begin (choose a book with a sturdy cover that allows it to remain

open when unlocked). Additionally, it is advisable that you select a book that is easily comprehensible and unfamiliar to you. This will greatly facilitate the examination process.

2. Please commence a timer for one minute on your mobile device or timepiece.

3. Commence reading from the designated point, continuing until the expiration of the allocated time frame, which is equivalent to 1 minute.

4. Please indicate in your book the exact location at which you concluded.

5. Please ascertain the quantity of lines within the section you have read.

6. Determine the quantity of words within the portion of text you have read, and then proceed to divide this number by the total number of lines present within said section. This calculation will

provide you with the mean value representing the number of words per line. Please approximate the outcome to the nearest integer value. Please calculate the product of this number and the lines you previously discovered. This is your outcome in terms of WPM (words per minute), alternatively known as your reading pace.

Avoid Any Distractions

Exclude any potential thoughts from your mind other than the content you are presently reading, irrespective of whether it is a conversation occurring in close proximity, the presence of a television nearby, the playing of loud music, or any other diverting activity.

In general, eliminate all distractions that could preoccupy your thoughts or undermine your ability to focus. It is imperative that you ensure your phone is set to silent mode, along with any other digital distractions that may disrupt your work, such as instant messengers that have the potential to alert you. Kindly inform your acquaintances that you will be temporarily unavailable online.

Whenever feasible, opt for a location where you can engage in uninterrupted reading. Through the process of honing your speed-reading skills, you will acquire the ability to focus effectively in a multitude of environments. To begin with, it is advised to read in a tranquil setting.

Regarding music, the preference is contingent upon one's individual disposition. Certain individuals manifest enhanced concentration abilities when engaging in tasks while listening to music, while others perceive music as a potential source of diversion. If one is accustomed to the practice of listening to music while engaged in the act of reading, and if said activity does not impede one's focus and attention, one may feel at liberty to proceed accordingly. Ensure that you maintain necessary provisions, such as water, in close proximity to prevent any disruptions to your focus during the course of your practice.

Have Purpose-Based Reading

Prior to proceeding with the consumption of a literary work or any written material, it is advisable to engage in introspection by posing inquiries to oneself. Such queries could encompass the nature of the literature being perused, the underlying purpose for engaging with the material, and whether the reading is being pursued purely for leisurely enjoyment. This practice of self-inquiry will serve as a valuable tool in ascertaining the primary motivation driving one's decision to approach the book in question. They will also assist you in developing a strategic approach that enhances your efficiency in reading.

When faced with unfamiliar content, the majority of readers exhibit a tendency to commence reading from the outset without further ado. This behavior is commonly observed in the majority of individuals. Nevertheless, when engaging with various forms of literature, this methodology is not optimal.

The presence of a discernible objective will facilitate your active engagement in the material you are perusing, thereby enhancing your reading speed. In the event that one does not actively involve themselves with the subject matter they are perusing, a sense of disinterest may arise, ultimately leading to a higher likelihood of reading at a sluggish pace. Active involvement with the material further enhances your focus, thereby facilitating a more comprehensive comprehension of the reading material.

Prior to commencing your reading of a book, it is advised to allocate a brief moment to articulate the objective of your reading. This objective will subsequently govern the manner in which you engross with the contents of the book.

Read The Key Chapter

During the process of conducting a preliminary read-through of your book, you may come across the primary sections within the text. In general, it can be observed that the majority of books tend to possess a few exceptional chapters that are interspersed with less substantive ones. If there are any parallels between the book you are currently engaged with and this particular aspect, locate the corresponding pivotal chapter.

As an illustration, in the event that the pivotal chapter of the book is the final chapter, it is advisable to commence by reading it. Engaging in such behavior does not violate any regulations. This provides you with an overarching understanding of the book prior to commencing. Following this, you may proceed with perusing the remainder of the book.

Stop Sub-Vocalizing

As previously mentioned within this literary work, the act of sub vocalizing, or audibly articulating words while reading, refers to the process of mentally hearing oneself engage in the act of reading. This technique represents the predominant method through which the majority of individuals acquire the skill of reading. Sub-vocalization constitutes a significant hindrance to the majority of individuals, impeding their ability to read at an optimal pace and impeding their progress in enhancing their reading speed. Altering this particular behavior poses a considerable challenge; however, it is indeed attainable. Enclosed herewith are several strategies that can be employed to address this particular habit.

Distract yourself

To mitigate subvocalization within cognitive processes, endeavor to divert the attention of the subconscious mind. What measures can be taken to accomplish this? An alternative course of action entails engaging in the act of masticating gum whilst perusing the written material. In the event that one engages in gum chewing while reading, it is possible for the act to divert one's attention away from the tendency to mentally recite words.

An alternative approach to diverting your attention is to employ an inner dialogue within your thoughts. You may also consider sequentially enumerating from one to three while engaging in the reading process. Divide each line into singular, dual, or triple segments. While engaging in this activity, it is essential to direct your gaze towards a fixed point situated at the commencement of a line, subsequently towards the middle of said line, and ultimately towards its termination.

As you consider these aspects, it is important to tally the occurrences. This will focus your gaze on a cluster of words as opposed to an individual word. This diverts your attention from articulating the words silently in your thoughts and enhances your reading pace (as you will be able to perceive multiple words in one instance instead of processing them individually). Initially, the utilization of this approach might prove perplexing. However, through consistent application, it gradually becomes more effortless.

An alternative approach to consider would be to engage in the examination of multiple words simultaneously, subsequently proceeding expediently. Begin by examining a group of two or three words, proceeding sequentially along the line to analyze the subsequent two or three words. Proceed forward after visually perceiving and comprehending the written words rather than audibly articulating the words and gradually augment your pace.

Enjoy listening to music

Engaging in the practice of listening to ambient music while reading not only diminishes subvocalization but can also enhance your level of focus in certain situations. Nevertheless, it is imperative to bear in mind that not all types of music facilitate concentration.

The recommendation is to listen to non-lyric music or even calm beats. This is due to the potential for other genres of music, specifically those that incorporate vocal elements, to pose a distraction while engaging in reading activities. For instance, you could opt to listen to instrumental or classical compositions. These genres of music enhance cognitive focus and foster the diminishment of subvocalization tendencies.

Commence adopting a more accelerated reading pace through intentional effort.

If your typical reading speed is approximately 250 words per minute, endeavor to increase your pace slightly beyond that range (around 300-500 words per minute). By exerting effort to read at a slightly accelerated pace, one can effectively reduce the mental verbalization of the words encountered while reading.

In addition, you will also enhance your concentration, as you will need to exercise greater attentiveness when reading at an accelerated pace. By diligently practicing reading at an accelerated pace, you will ultimately enhance your reading efficiency.

Avoid Regressions

Instances of regression occur when one engages in redundant perusal of written content. Occasionally, one might develop the tendency to engage in the act of revisiting previously read words, and in certain instances, they may find themselves backtracking a few sentences in order to verify their comprehension.

Continuing to regress adversely impacts your reading speed, thereby elongating the time required for comprehension. Additionally, it results in the disruption of the text's structure and flow. Additionally, it is possible that you might diminish your comprehension of the topic. Hence, when engaged in the act of reading, refrain from recalling a few words or sentences unless an imperative need arises.

To mitigate the rate of regression, endeavor to employ the self-pacing techniques delineated in the subsequent phase as you peruse.

Avoid Reading Word-By-Word

Reading in a meticulous manner not only diminishes reading speed but also results in the inadvertent omission of crucial information. When engaging in rapid reading, you are capable of perceiving numerous words in a single glance or grouping them together, enhancing your comprehension and assimilation capabilities. As previously mentioned in the section on diverting one's attention, it is advisable to consider multiple words simultaneously and progressively augment the quantity.

By engaging in the practice of increasing the number of words you comprehend per unit of time, you will be able to circumvent this tendency of reading in a word-by-word manner. One can enhance the quantity of words perceived in a solitary glance by augmenting the distance separating one's eyes and the reading material. As a result of this, your visual field will expand, thereby enabling you to perceive a greater number of words within a single glance.

The greater the number of words apprehended within a single glance, the swifter the pace of one's reading.

Utilize Speed Reading Software

There exists a wide range of speed-reading software options accessible across all platforms. These software applications have the potential to enhance one's reading speed.

Machine-assisted speed-reading entails the utilization of various methodologies, such as employing a pointer for meta guiding, incorporating guided reading exercises, and employing RSVP (Rapid Serial Visual Presentation)." In addition, certain software platforms employ a technique known as rapid succession to enhance your reading speed beyond the average rate of 250 words per minute.

Speed Reading Is Beneficial For Cognitive Development

Presented below is an extensive analysis elucidating the advantages of Speed Reading on the cognitive functions of the human brain:

Improved Memory. The brain can be likened to a muscle. By engaging in cognitive exercises, our brains can be strengthened, thereby enhancing their performance capabilities. Engaging in Speed Reading encourages our cognitive faculties to operate at an elevated capacity. When you cultivate cognitive abilities to enhance the speed at which your brain absorbs information, you can anticipate concomitant improvements in other cognitive capacities, including but not limited to memory. When engaging in Speed Reading, the cognitive function of memory functions akin to a stabilizing muscle.

Better Focus. The majority of individuals possess a capability to read a minimum of 200 words per minute, thereby encompassing the standard reading speed. However, there are individuals who possess the ability to read as fast as 300 words per minute. What is the reason behind such a substantial disparity? There are two main factors that contribute to this. Firstly, the conventional approach to reading that is typically instructed to us lacks efficiency. Another factor contributing to this issue is a lack of concentration. Failure to maintain concentration and attentiveness while reading could potentially result in the dispersion of our thoughts and the subsequent preoccupation with unrelated matters. Speed reading cultivates concentration.

Higher levels Of Self-Confidence. I am of the opinion that this outcome can be attributed to the recognition that once one possesses the skill to read faster and comprehend more, they are capable of acquiring knowledge in various domains at an accelerated pace. As you enhance your proficiency in reading and accelerate your learning pace, you will witness an expansion of opportunities and a broadening of horizons in your life. This phenomenon occurs because each literary piece, regardless of its genre, be it a work of fiction or nonfiction, serves to expand our consciousness, granting us a newfound capacity to perceive greater complexity and meaning within our own existence. This newly discovered profundity enhances our level of self-assurance.

Improved Logic. Engaging in reading provides mental stimulation and enhances cognitive abilities. When individuals develop the cognitive ability to enhance their reading speed, a remarkable phenomenon occurs. Your cognitive function improves as your brain enhances its ability to organize data and establish connections among stored information. As you enhance your reading speed, the swifter this progression occurs, leading to a discernible enhancement in your logical aptitude as you adapt to swiftly responding to matters that previously required more time for comprehension.

Emotional Well-being. Reading generally provides a profoundly calming experience. It possesses the potential to alleviate stress by diverting the mind from the burdensome concerns and detrimental thoughts. By increasing your reading speed, your immersion in the material will be enhanced. This leads to a predominant concentration on the information being read. This phenomenon is commonly referred to as active meditation. Active-meditation is an introspective state attained through the engagement in a specific undertaking. This province has the capacity to alleviate stress and enhance one's emotional welfare.

Chapter 5: Enhance Your Reading Experience with Four Easy Strategies

"So, what are your current sentiments towards reading?" This is a crucial inquiry that demands attention.

The manner in which you perceive and handle reading can be influenced by your emotional disposition towards it.

If you belong to the group of individuals who harbor ambivalent sentiments regarding reading or harbor a dislike for the activity, yet are compelled to engage in it out of necessity, it is imperative that you acquire some helpful strategies and techniques to transform your reading into an enjoyable endeavor.

For those individuals who belong to the category of people who derive pleasure from the act of reading, the provided tips can be seen as supplementary benefits!

Recommendation #1: Select an appropriate location and time for engaging in reading activities.

Do you enjoy indulging in a cozy and comfortable reading experience on the couch at your friend's residence? Or does the concept of reading in bed induce drowsiness?

Does the atmosphere of a coffee shop have a calming and stimulating effect on your capacity to engage in reading? Alternatively, are you experiencing a sense of diversion as a result of the individuals in your vicinity?

Can a tranquil public space such as a library contribute to your ability to concentrate?

The main idea at hand is that individuals vary in their preferences and habits, regardless of whether they choose to read physical copies or digital versions. In order to optimize their reading experience, it is recommended to select a conducive environment that is devoid of interruptions, provides a comfortable setting, and offers adequate lighting conditions.

Make an effort to visit your preferred location on a weekly basis.

Recommendation #2: Select an opportune moment for engaging in reading activities.

The timing at which one engages in document reading plays a pivotal role in both the comprehension and the retention of the information acquired. If you encounter a text that is laborious or demands significant focus, it is preferable to approach it during the early hours of the day. This is when your mind is invigorated, the surrounding environment is tranquil, and you possess the highest levels of energy.

Impose stringent constraints upon your reading commitments. Establish for yourself a restriction of no longer than 40-50 minutes of continuous reading.

Recommendation #3: Select the appropriate reading material

Select the appropriate text to peruse. Please consider purchasing a captivating reading material, even if it happens to be a comic. The more vibrant, light-hearted, or thought-provoking it is, the more commendable it becomes. Peruse it and derive pleasure from it, ceasing your engagement once disinterest arises.

Suggestion #4: Enhance your reading experience through a mutual support system

Attempt to foster a friend or partner's interest in perusing the same literary selection as yourself, subsequently engaging in a thoughtful discourse regarding the content.

These fundamental strategies for reading comprehension will prove advantageous in the realms of higher education, professional endeavors, and personal spheres.

Chapter 4: Enhancing Information Retention

Enhancing information retention requires a delicate equilibrium between honing one's speed reading abilities and accurately reproducing the information, using one's own phrasing, internally. Numerous factors impede the pace of one's reading, including subvocalization and sentence regression, thereby impacting the extent to which information is retained. When excessive emphasis is placed on the main point of a sentence, it not only results in a decrease in reading speed for the individual, but also introduces extraneous information that hampers cognitive clarity. This is a common occurrence wherein individuals devote extensive hours to studying yet fail to grasp the essence or main points relayed in the text.

Due to their excessive concentration on individual sentences rather than considering the entirety of the paragraph, so to speak.

The primary objective of speed reading is to facilitate the long-term retention and retrieval of information. Numerous individuals hold the assertion that the correlation between these two notions is robust: if one possesses the ability to engage in rapid reading, they are capable of enhancing their cognitive capacity to assimilate information more swiftly and retain it more effectively. However, this assumption is incorrect. Succeeding in speed reading entails the ability to read quickly, whereas enhancing information retention refers to the capacity to retain the information that is being read at a fast pace. Both activities involve distinct sets of exercises and require varying durations to develop and master.

The fundamental tenet underlying the concept of memory rests on the notion that our recollection is contingent upon our cognitive focus and contemplation. This is the rationale behind individuals who inscribe annotations in the margins of books, underscore relevant content, and even record the comprehensive insights in their personal notebooks and workbooks. Nevertheless, such strategies tend to be unproductive as they divert attention away from grasping the overarching purpose of the section or chapter, resulting in an excessive fixation on the words being highlighted. The individual's cognitive focus shifts towards the memorization of words rather than the comprehension of their significance, resulting in the ability to recite the content from the workbook without effectively employing it in the relevant contexts.

Which, strictly speaking, does not align with the definition of learning. That can be described as a thoughtless repetition.

The primary factor contributing significantly to memory retention in the context of speed reading lies in the individual's capacity to rephrase information using their own wording. Do you recall the SQ3R method that was previously mentioned within the text? One of the primary elements involves paraphrasing the content that you have read. This particular phase holds great significance as it aligns perfectly with the underlying theoretical principle of memory, necessitating cognitive engagement with the subject matter.

Speed reading does not entail heightened rates of information processing. The concept of speed reading entails employing various techniques and using pacers to increase the rate at which one can comprehend and process written material. The ability to retain and process information is a distinct aspect that necessitates deliberate practice in order to derive its advantages. It is achievable to engage in rapid reading but fail to appropriately retain the acquired information.

This is the reason why it is essential to verbally articulate information using your own phrasing.

There are alternative actions beyond speed reading and recitation that have the potential to enhance memory retention, and they involve nurturing one's cognitive faculties in other realms. Firstly, it is imperative that your brain receives sufficient oxygen in order to sustain its optimal function and facilitate the necessary neural networking processes. In a manner similar to how the human body necessitates the consumption of water and food in order to sustain its various functionalities, the brain relies on the consumption of oxygen and water to maintain its ongoing operation. Engaging in mindful breathing exercises and maintaining proper hydration can provide the necessary sustenance for your brain to sustain the process of synthesizing these connections. Ensure that you are equipped with a bottle of water while engaging in the practice of speed reading, and make a point to hydrate yourself at regular intervals. Incorporate some breathing exercises into the process of reciting the information to oneself. Not only will these augment cognitive function, but they will mitigate stress levels, thereby enhancing the efficacy of the information assimilated in your neural network pathways.

Furthermore, it is important to note that an elevation in both water and oxygen levels has the potential to enhance blood circulation. Consequently, this can greatly facilitate the formation and acceleration of neuronal connections. Increased blood circulation leads to a more efficient delivery of essential nutrients, resulting in enhanced overall bodily functioning.

For certain individuals, the concept of engaging in self-dialogue to process information may seem absurd or engender a sense of isolation. Consequently, engage in a conversation with an acquaintance. Enlist the assistance of an individual who is also engaged in studying the same material, or someone who is willing to serve as a sounding board, and engage in a verbal discussion to further comprehend and digest the information. Social support plays a vital role in stress management, with numerous studies demonstrating that extended periods of profound loneliness can have detrimental effects on both physical health and the immune system, ultimately resulting in illness. Certain individuals may find that their learning experience is enhanced when in the presence of others, and engaging in speed reading to improve information retention does not necessarily have to be a solitary endeavor. If you are an individual who thrives in a social setting for the purpose of relaxation or enhanced learning, then it is advised to be in a more sociable environment while engaging in speed reading and information retention activities. It can be concluded with ease!

Nevertheless, the information you are currently holding onto will be rendered ineffective if your mind is unable to find respite, a crucial component for establishing these associations. Reciting the information stimulates the activation of developing neural pathways, however, it is only when the body is in a state of rest that the brain can gather sufficient energy to effectively extend its connections to adjacent neurons and establish meaningful links with them. Obtain the necessary amount of sleep, and your brain will establish connections and retrieve information at its highest level of effectiveness. However, should you deprive your brain of the necessary amount of sleep, it will greatly diminish your ability to retain information and maintain focus while engaging in speed reading. This decline in cognitive performance can subsequently result in feelings of frustration and ultimately contribute to heightened bodily stress. This repetitive pattern of devastation persists akin to a substantial paradox, ultimately leading to a point where one becomes uncertain how to extricate themselves from it, often resulting in complete renunciation of the artistic pursuit.

Ensure you obtain the necessary restorative rest. It is essential for the consolidation of your memory.

Additionally, one should never underestimate the efficacy of taking a respite. The cognitive functions of your brain persist even in the absence of immediate concentration on a particular undertaking. Numerous studies conducted have demonstrated that the human brain exhibits a tendency to remember information better when it is presented at the beginning and end, a phenomenon commonly referred to as the primacy and recency effects. By incorporating regular intervals of rest, you are effectively amplifying the occurrence of beginnings and endings, thereby enabling you to exploit this innate cognitive phenomenon as a strategic physiological tool. Not solely will you have the opportunity to obtain a period of rest during your information processing session, but your mind will also have the capacity to make more frequent use of this occurrence, which may consequently lead to increased overall retention of information.

Another cognitive phenomenon that has been identified is known as the Zeigarnik Effect. This effect posits that individuals who are interrupted while engaged in a learning task before completing it are more likely to remember and retain information related to that task compared to those who successfully complete it without any interruption. It may seem unconventional, yet that phenomenon is capitalizing on the characteristics of the primacy and recency effect. By integrating regular intervals for rest, one can substantially enhance their capacity to retain a greater quantity of information.

Keep in mind that your brain is fundamentally akin to a muscle: the greater the degree to which you exercise it, the more optimal, robust, and proficient it will grow. By engaging in cognitive exercises and pursuing activities that bring joy and intellectually stimulate oneself, the brain releases endorphins that can enhance one's overall sense of wellness. Additionally, these have the potential to alleviate physical discomfort, bolster the immune system, and mitigate the occurrence of depressive episodes. The release of these endorphins can mitigate the general impact of stress, a phenomenon that ultimately contributes to the deterioration and unraveling of neuronal pathways. Therefore, it is crucial to diligently manage and minimize stress in order to optimize information retention. Partake in activities that stimulate your mental faculties, such as indulging in literature, embarking on strolls outdoors, or engaging in specialized mathematical and verbal puzzles. These activities will not only revitalize your spirits but also enhance your capacity to retain information effectively.

However, the concept of perceiving the brain as a muscle gives rise to other factors that induce alterations in it, which are not beneficial. In the same vein as prioritizing the provision of essential nourishment for the mind, it is equally paramount to refrain from exposing it to superfluous elements. The usage of nicotine, recreational drugs, caffeine, and any other transient substances that alter the mind will profoundly influence the cognitive ability of the brain to retain information, and may even impede its capacity for information retention. Nurturing both your physical well-being and cognitive functions necessitates exercising caution not only in selecting what you consume, but also in what you abstain from.

However, this extends beyond addictive substances. Even rudimentary substances like antibiotics have the capacity to transiently modify cognitive information processing and retention, by impeding the innate sleep process, diminishing the duration of essential REM sleep required for cerebral rejuvenation, and even suppressing appetite. All of these factors lead to modifications and repercussions in your brain, exerting a detrimental influence on its capacity for information processing and retention.

A final piece of counsel for optimizing the retention of information is to ensure that you establish a sense of organization in your approach. Filling your mind with extraneous information is akin to haphazardly adding miscellaneous items to your storage space. Why? The greater the number of items you deposit into your wardrobe, the more limited the space becomes for storing essential items like garments and footwear. To create space within the room, it is necessary to organize and remove unnecessary items from your closet, repositioning them in alternate locations. This process demands a considerable amount of time and effort.

If one were to occupy their mind with superfluous information that is not necessary, significant amounts of mental rearrangement become necessary in order to effectively retain desired information. This considerably depletes the cognitive resources of the brain on a daily basis, thereby adversely impacting your ability to effectively absorb the necessary information.

Ultimately, although speed reading incorporates specific techniques, the key to retaining information lies in the recitation of knowledge and the practice of adopting beneficial habits to maintain cognitive functionality. It possesses a higher level of abstraction, rendering it potentially one of the most exasperating endeavors for individuals seeking to cultivate the skill.

However, akin to comprehending the gradual development of reading skills lending itself to enhanced reading speed, comprehending the initial cognitive mechanisms of information absorption and retrieval will foster a deeper understanding of the learning process undertaken by the brain. Furthermore, this comprehension will provide valuable insights on how to effectively harness the brain's neuroplasticity for personal gain.

www.ingramcontent.com/pod-product-compliance
Lightning Source LLC
Chambersburg PA
CBHW050241120526
44590CB00016B/2178